Language: English

ISBN: 979-8-9884988-6-5

INTRODUCTION TO **HOPE**

Thank you for choosing hope and participating in Hopeful Mindsets.

This is the first step on your hope journey. Hope is a teachable, measurable, and learnable skill that can have positive ramifications on every aspect of your life. Higher hope is associated with greater emotional and psychological well-being, economic security, improved academic performance, less violence, less loneliness, and enhanced personal relationships.

Yet we are never taught what hope is or how to activate hope in our lives.

We often think of hope as a "wish," but hope is so much more than that. We define hope as a vision for something in your future, fueled by both positive feelings and inspired actions. Both feelings and actions are critical to hope; actions are what differentiate hope from a "wish."

We cannot make you hopeful. However, the lessons contained in this book can teach you the "how-to" of hope, and give you the critical hope skills you can use to activate hope in your life and the lives of those around you.

Your hope journey is up to you. The more you use the skills outlined in this workbook, the easier it will be to manage hopelessness and return to hope.

Welcome to the Hopeful Mindsets community.

We would like to thank the following people for their contribution to our programs:

This program would not be possible without the brilliant leadership, support, and commitment to hope by:

Myron L. Belfer MD, MPA, Harvard Catalyst

Myron is Professor of Psychiatry in the Department of Psychiatry, Children's Hospital Boston, Harvard Medical School, and Senior Associate in Psychiatry at the Children's Hospital of Boston. Dr. Belfer is a Champion for Hope.

Kathryn Goetzke MBA, Author, Creator
Contributors: Taylor Steed, Katharine Lee-Kramer, Veronica O,Brien
Sarah Mellen, Mic Fariscal, Anna Termulo Montances and **Naneth Samoya-Jumawid**

To our advisors, hope contributors, and experts: .
Dr. Edward Barksdale, Dr. Frank Gard Jameson, Mayor Hillary Schieve, Kristy L. Stark M.A., Ed.M., BCBA, Karen Kirby PhD, MSc, BSc, C.Psychol, AfBPS, SFHEA, Ulster University, **Marie Dunne and the Northern Ireland** team that helped plant the seeds for this work.

Pioneers in early Hope Science including **Dr. Crystal Bryce, Dr. Dan Tomasulo, Dr. Chan Heliman, Dr. Matthew Gallagher, Dr. Jennifer Cheavens** and the late **Dr. Shane Lopez.**

iFred Board of Directors:
Tom Dean, Susan Minamyer, Jim Link, Dr. John Grohol, Kathryn Goetzke, Dr. Mindy Magrane

The Hopeful Minds Advisory Board

Some of our early funders: Sutter Health, Anthem, The Gordon Family Giving Fund of the Parasol Tahoe Community Foundation, The Shine Hope Company, and The Mood Factory.

IN SPECIAL RECOGNITION
Susan Minamyer, whose unconditional love, support, encouragement, faith, and brilliance planted and watered the seeds necessary to create and grow this program. Kathryn's big brothers **Arnold and Fred, and Clara, Maura, Jack, Sophie, Charles, and Sarah,** who continue to strengthen, build, and inspire Kathryn's hope.

IN HONOR
In recognition of all in the world that struggled with hopelessness in some way, shape or form, and left us way too early, including a few close to our hearts. Thank you for teaching us so much about life, love, and hope. May we spread Hope far and wide in your name and honor:
Jon and Sally Goetzke, Tom Foorman, Dr. Stephen C. Gleason, Vicky Harrison, Eloise Land, Jesse Lewis, and Austin Weirich.

TABLE OF CONTENTS

COMMON TERMS FOR HOPEFUL MINDSETS

The most important terms we use in this workbook, and that we hope you begin to use in your daily life, include:

HOPE: We define hope as a vision for something in the future, fueled by both positive feelings and inspired actions.

HOPELESSNESS: Hopelessness is both a feeling of despair and a sense of helplessness. It is emotional (a negative feeling) and motivational (an inability to act). We all experience moments of hopelessness and manage them with hope skills.

POSITIVE FEELINGS: Positive feelings are those feelings that help us to stay hopeful as we work towards our goals.

INSPIRED ACTIONS: Inspired actions are the deliberate steps you take to get in your upstairs brains and toward your goals in life.

UPSTAIRS BRAIN: This is where our thinking, imagining, problem-solving, and learning occur. This part of the brain is responsible for the development of sound decision-making and planning, control over emotions and body, and self-understanding and empathy. The upstairs brain is also where we access our positive feelings.

DOWNSTAIRS BRAIN: Also referred to as the reptilian brain, this part of the brain is responsible for basic functions such as breathing, blinking, heart rate, and fight, flight, freeze, or fawn mode. It is also responsible for the chemical stimulus associated with strong emotions, such as anger, sadness, and fear.

STRESS RESPONSE: Your stress response is when an external or internal trigger causes your brain to release stress hormones, such as cortisol, adrenaline, and norepinephrine, that force you into your fight, flight, freeze, or fawn mode. It generally lasts 90 seconds from time of the last trigger.

STRESS SKILLS: These are actions that help you navigate your stress response and work through your body's chemical response to external stimuli, to get manage your downstairs brain and get you back upstairs.

HAPPINESS HABITS: These are healthy, long-term habits that help you stay in your upstairs brain, where you access the problem-solving skills, collaboration, and passion, all critical for hope. When you take time for Happiness Habits, your brain releases happiness hormones, such as endorphins, dopamine, serotonin, and oxytocin.

NOURISHING NETWORKS: Your Nourishing Networks are the Hope Networks of the people in your life that provide you with support, help you stay on track, encourage you to succeed, and who you do the same for in return.

ELIMINATING CHALLENGES: Challenges to Hope are negative thinking patterns, like limiting beliefs, automatic negative thoughts, all-or-nothing thinking, negative bias, rumination, worry, focusing on uncontrollables, attaching to outcomes, and internalizing failure, that can keep us in hopelessness states. Eliminating challenges are the conscious act of using hope skills to overcome these challenges and get back to hope.

THE HOPE MATRIX: The Hope Matrix is the process that we use to get from hopelessness to hope. The Hope Matrix teaches us that to cultivate hope, we must move from despair to positive feelings, and from helplessness to inspired actions.

Shine Hope™: This is the mnemonic we use to remember our hope skills. Shine stands for: **S**tress Skills, **H**appiness Habits, **I**nspired Actions, **N**ourishing Networks, and **E**liminating Challenges and is what we use to activate skills for hope.

Additionally, you will learn how our Shine Hope framework helps you move from a moment of HOPELESSNESS to HOPE

THE HOPE MATRIX

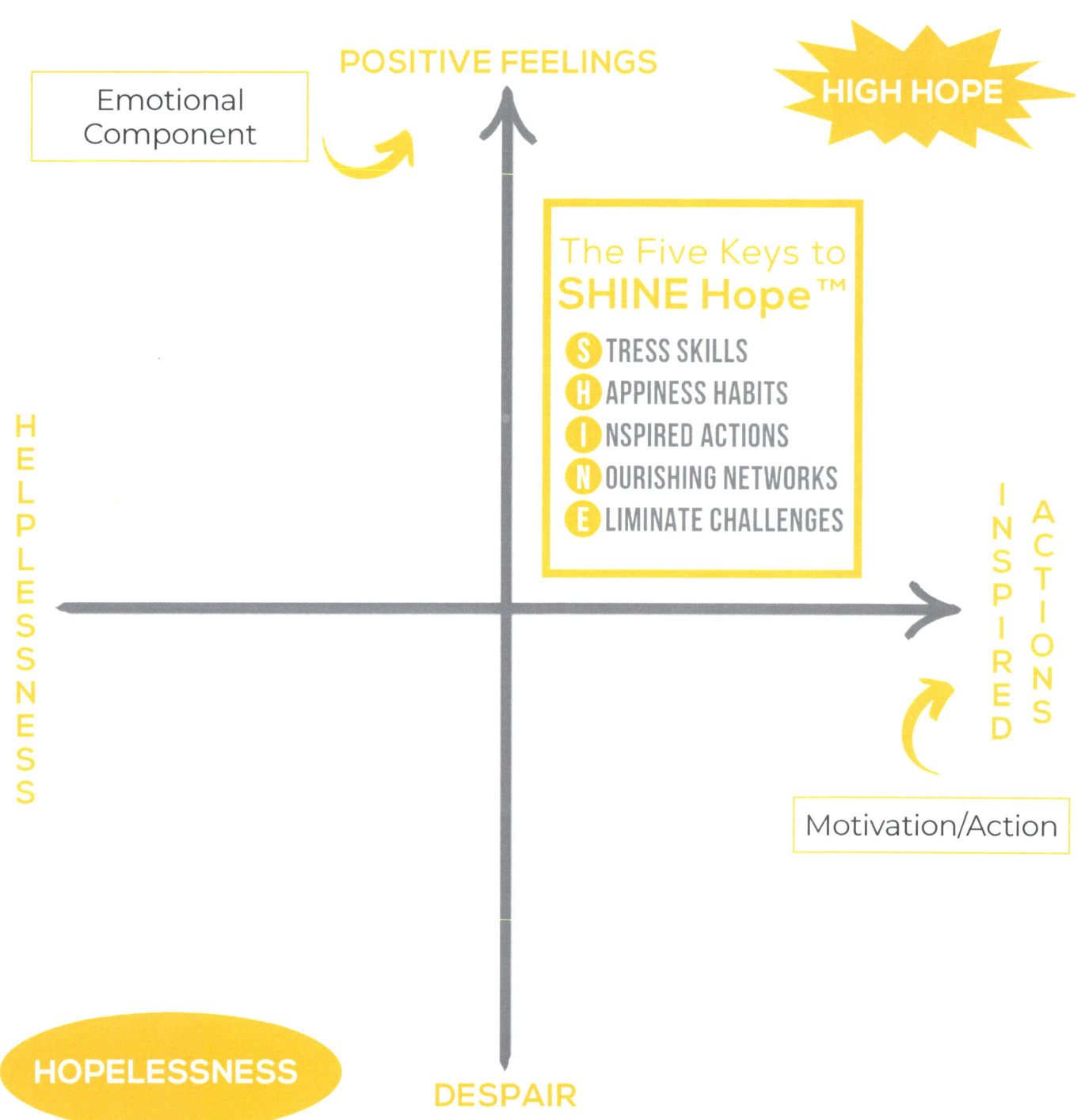

POSITIVE FEELINGS

Emotional Component

HIGH HOPE

The Five Keys to SHINE Hope™

STRESS SKILLS
HAPPINESS HABITS
INSPIRED ACTIONS
NOURISHING NETWORKS
ELIMINATE CHALLENGES

HELPLESSNESS

INSPIRED ACTIONS

Motivation/Action

HOPELESSNESS

DESPAIR

THE HOPE MATRIX

The Hope Matrix is the process that we use to get from hopelessness to hope. The Hope Matrix teaches us that to reach hopeful mindset, we must move from despair to positive feelings, and from helplessness to inspired actions.

Directions: Fill in the blanks below with the following words: **Hope, Hopelessness, Despair, Helplessness, Positive Feelings, Inspired Actions.**

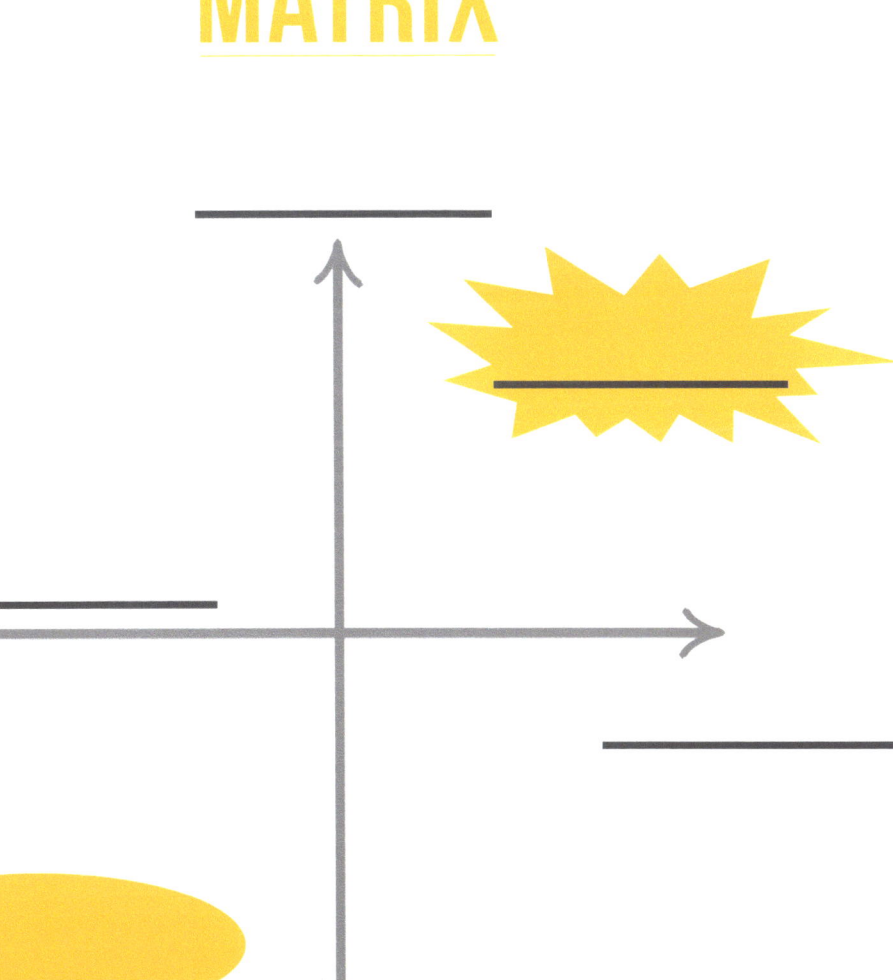

HOPE SCALES

Your hope score is a tool for you to use to monitor your progress, track your hope journey, and reflect on how hopeful you are in the current moment. Hope is not fixed; when you practice hope skills, you can improve your hope score.

Use the link provided to take the Snyder Hope Scale Assessment:

www.theshinehopecompany.com/measure-your-hope

My Current Snyder Hope Scale Score: _____

How do you feel about your score?

_____

_____

How hopeful have you been in your life?

_____

_____

How has your hope level impacted your ability to achieve goals?

_____

_____

In what areas of your life do you feel like you could be more hopeful?

_____

_____

This course teaches you the hope skills you can use to create, maintain, and grow hope. There will be times throughout your life when you or someone you love experiences hopelessness. It is at these times, when your hope score is at its lowest, that it is most important to practice skills to activate hope.

The goal of this course is to learn the "how-to" of hope so that you can both create a model for your own life and share the power of hope with others.

Who in your life could benefit from higher hope?

_____

_____

_____

_____

What organizations or businesses in your community could benefit from learning about hope?

_____

_____

_____

_____

STRENGTHS FINDER

Understanding your strengths is important for creating and maintaining hope. Focusing on your strengths can help you manage your stress response, cultivate positive thoughts, and focus on the future. As you continue through this workbook, you will repeatedly be asked to reflect on your strengths.

Take a moment to learn more about your strengths by taking the free VIA Character Strengths Survey here:

theshinehopecompany.pro.viasurvey.org 🔍

Write down the top five strengths identified in your results:

1 _____

2 _____

3 _____

4 _____

5 _____

Which of these strengths do you think is most tied to your ability to maintain hope?

_____

_____

_____

_____

Are you activating your strengths regularly? How so?

_____

_____

_____

_____

How can you better utilize your strengths at home? At work? At School?

_____

_____

_____

_____

WHAT IS YOUR WHY?

Have you ever thought about your reasoning for choosing the career path you're on? Understanding your why makes it easier to focus on your core values, which make it easier to accomplish goals. Additionally, understanding your why can help you when you are faced with feelings of hopelessness in life. Let's explore your why now:

What is your 'why' in the workplace? Why do you want to work here? What motivates you to be involved in this position? Why do you care about this work? What is your 'why'?

_____

_____

Now that you have your initial why, let's dig deeper. Oftentimes the true why that is linked to values comes when we think a little deeper about why we are participating in certain work.

What is your why to your above answer?

_____

_____

What is your why to your above answer?

_____

_____

What is your why to your above answer?

_____

_____

Is that your final WHY? If not, what is your why to your above answer?

_____

_____

When things get hard, it is important to come back to your final why. This is WHY you are doing this work. This is why the work is important. Your why needs to anchor you in challenging times.

SHINE HOPE™

A HOW-TO FOR HOPE IN TRYING TIMES

Scan the code to measure hope with the **Hope Scale!**

S TRESS SKILLS	H APPINESS HABITS	I NSPIRED ACTIONS	N OURISHING NETWORKS	E LIMINATING CHALLENGES
90 second pause	Activating purpose	WOOP process	5:1 Rule	Limiting beliefs
Belly breathing	Pursuing passion	SMART goals	Compassion	Automatic Negative Thoughts (ANTs)
Journaling	Utilizing strengths	Stretch goals	Forgiveness	All-or-nothing thinking
Gardening	Meditation	Achievement goals	Love	Negative bias
Calming music	Smiling	Intrinsic goals	Gratitude	Rumination & Worry
Affirming beliefs	Exercising / Nutrition	Mastery goals	Recognition	Focusing on Uncontrollables
Sensory engagement	Creating / listening to music	Micro goals / Stepping	Support	Attaching to outcomes
Cold plunge	Dancing / Singing	Habit Stacking	Faith	Internalizing failure
Decluttering	Drawing / Painting	Visualization	Trust	Toxic Consumption
Prayer	Gratitude	Overcoming obstacles	Respect	Nocebo Effect
Nature walk	Volunteering	Regoaling	Effective Listening	Mind Wandering
Napping	Wonder/Awe	Write down goals / check in	Empathy	Implicity Bias
Laughter	Quality sleep		Kindness	Negative Framing
Crying	Doodling		Animals	Perfectionism
Tapping				Taking things personally
Yoga				
Mantras				

the **shine hope**™ company

© The Shine Hope Company, LLC

STRESS SKILLS

Stress Skills are actions that help you navigate your stress response and work through your body's chemical response to external stimuli. By practicing them, you are teaching yourself how to proactively manage the emotional despair found in hopelessness and move towards positive feelings where you activate hope.

The Stress Response

This is when you are emotionally triggered by something in your environment, and you go into fight, flight, freeze, or fawn mode as your body releases stress hormones, such as cortisol, adrenaline, and norepinephrine. You are in your downstairs brain, and can't reach your upstairs brain; the upstairs brain is the place where you make good decisions for moving towards all you hope for in life.

90 second pause	Sensory engagement	Laughter
Belly breathing	Cold plunge	Crying
Journaling	Decluttering	Tapping
Gardening	Prayer	Yoga
Calming music	Nature walk	Mantras
Affirming beliefs	Napping	

STRESS **SKILLS**

The First Key to Shine Hope is identifying and managing your stress response using Stress Skills.

It's important to understand the connection between your brain, body, and behavior so you can begin to use it to your advantage. When your mood changes, it may be so subtle that you don't pick up on it at first. However, your body does, and it reacts. These are known as psychosomatic responses. For example, when I am triggered, I grind my teeth, my shoulders clench, and I sometimes even forget to breathe. All of these reactions are caused by the relationship between my brain and biology.

The relationship between your body and brain is woven by complex circuitry, meaning that they influence one another in various ways that can be hard to identify in our own lives. Psychosomatic responses are manifestations of the state of your brain in your physical body, they can come in the form of discomfort, sensations, or habits. Behavior under stress is often the culmination of thoughts and feelings, and while this can sometimes seem problematic, like when you snap at someone because you are stressed, it can also be incredibly beneficial. When you look at the connection between your brain, biology, and behavior through the lens of hope, you can start to reframe how you think and feel.

Increasing hope isn't just about influencing your brain; it is also about positively impacting your biology and behavior. When you positively impact your brain, you are also providing long-term benefits.

THE DOWNSTAIRS BRAIN. The downstairs brain, also known as the amygdala, includes the limbic region and brainstem. It is the more primitive part of the brain (also referred to as the reptilian brain), and is responsible for basic functions such as breathing, blinking, heart rate, and fight, flight, or freeze mode. The downstairs brain is also responsible for the chemical stimulus associated with strong emotions, such as anger, rage, sadness, frustration, and fear.

THE UPSTAIRS BRAIN. Your upstairs brain is also known as the prefrontal cortex. It is where your thinking, imagining, learning, problem-solving, and creativity all occur. This part of your brain is responsible for the development of sound decision-making and planning, self-understanding, and empathy. The upstairs brain is also where you feel positive emotions, such as happiness, contentment, peace, and passion. You may remember that positive feelings are the first ingredient of hope; this means that you can only access your hope when you are in your upstairs brain.

It's important to remember that the downstairs brain is not a "bad" part of your brain. It is important for survival and it helps us understand the world around us. However, you don't want to be in your downstairs brain all the time. The hope skills you are going to learn during this program will help you move from your downstairs brain into your upstairs brain so that you can always return to a hopeful mindset.

MY BRAIN

Fill in the blanks with the emotions of the emoticon facial expressions that match using *fear, anger, sadness, relaxed, happy, and excited.*

STOP. *BREATHE.* RELAX.

Directions: Circle your top four favorite stress skills from the list below. If there are additional Stress Skills you use that are not on the list, use the space below the add them.

Stress Skills

- 90 Second Pause
- Deep breathing exercises
- Meditation
- Sleep
- Listening to calming music
- Spending time in nature
- Focusing on our 5 senses
- Visualization
- Drawing
- Decluttering
- Scream into Pillow

- Gardening
- Writing in a journal
- Putting on a play
- Playing sports
- Talking to a trusted friend or adult
- Helping someone else
- Watching a funny video
- Any other actions that help you calm down

MY FAVORITE STRESS SKILLS

-
-
-
-
-
-
-
-

-
-
-
-
-
-
-

STRESS RESPONSE

Dr. Jill Bolte Taylor developed the 90-second rule in her book, "My Stroke of Insight," to explain the biology behind your stress response. The 90-second rule says that when you are triggered by something in your environment, a chemical process takes place in your body for approximately 90 seconds. For 90 seconds after the environmental trigger, your body is flooded with stress hormones, such as cortisol, adrenaline, and norepinephrine.

When you experience your stress response, you are in your downstairs brain, and can't reach your upstairs brain; the upstairs brain is the place where you make good decisions for moving towards all you hope for in life.

Your ability to learn to proactively control this response is the First Key to Shine Hope, because it is what empowers you to start controlling how you react to triggers in your environment. Are you controlling them, or are your triggers and other people controlling you?

You give others power over you every time you react to something someone else does or allow someone to "trigger" you. If they are trying to get a negative reaction from you and they succeed, you ultimately lose. When you learn to control your triggers and reactions, you are able to move into and remain in the upstairs brain.

You can manage your stress response using Stress Skills. By practicing Stress Skills, you are teaching yourself how to proactively manage the emotional despair found in hopelessness and move towards positive feelings where you activate hope.

STRESS SKILLS: DEEP BREATHING ACTIVITY

One Stress Skill you can practice anywhere is deep belly breathing. Belly breathing differs from typical breathing because it encourages full oxygen exchange, meaning it allows the body to fully trade carbon dioxide with incoming oxygen. Additionally, belly breathing slows the heart rate and lowers blood pressure, which are two physiological processes that are strained during increased stress.

Today, I want you to intentionally practice deep belly breathing at least five times throughout the day, for at least 90 seconds each time. If you can, take your deep breaths when you feel yourself sinking into your downstairs brain or you feel the stress response kicking in.

As you take your deep breaths, follow these steps:

- Sit in a comfortable position with your back as straight as possible.
- Notice how your body feels. Take a few seconds to just relax. Relax your neck, shoulders, arms, legs, and feet. Can you feel your heartbeat? Can you sense your breath? Try a few big inhales and exhales.
- When you're ready, place one hand on your chest and the other on your belly button (below the rib cage).
- Now take a long, slow, deep breath, in through your nose for a count of 10 (or as long as you are able). As you breathe in, you want to send the air to your belly button. Your hand on your belly should rise while the hand on your chest remains still.
- Once you get to 10, slowly exhale out of your mouth. Feel the muscles of your stomach tighten and your hand lower.
- Do this for at least 90 seconds (or 10 slow, deep breaths).

As you breathe, pay attention to how your brain and body feel before, during, and after the deep breathing.

How did you feel before taking the deep breaths? How did you feel after?

_____

_____

_____

_____

Make sure you use a stopwatch to time your breathing so you can experience the full 90-seconds. This is the amount of time it takes the stress hormones to cycle through your system after you experience a trigger.

REFLECTION QUESTIONS

How does your stress impact your goals?

_____
_____
_____
_____

Why is managing stress important for hope?

_____
_____
_____
_____

How is stress impacting your performance at work?

_____
_____
_____
_____

How can you more positively manage your stress in the office?

_____
_____
_____
_____

How can you notice when colleagues are in upstairs and downstairs brain?

_____
_____
_____
_____

How can you more proactively interact with them during those times?

_____
_____
_____
_____

IDENTIFYING YOUR **FEELINGS**

The three main emotions associated with despair (the emotional component of hopelessness) are anger, fear, and sadness. When we are emotionally triggered, sadness, anger, and/or fear can activate our despair and cause us to move towards our downstairs brain.

However, we shouldn't simply push these emotions away, as that often leads to harmful behaviors, such as addiction, violence, and self-harm. It is important that when we feel despair, we proactively acknowledge the feeling, identify the root emotions that are causing the despair, and discover what they are telling us. Only once we have honored, experienced, explored, and learned from the emotion can we fully release it.

Using the questions below, think about the last time you experienced each of these emotions, and start to explore how you feel these emotions and express them.

ANGER

Describe the last time you were angry:

_____

How did you experience anger in your mind? _____

How did you experience anger in your body? _____

How did you respond when you were angry?

_____

What did your anger tell you about your environment or yourself?

_____

What are unhealthy ways you respond to anger? _____

What are healthy ways you respond to anger? _____

SADNESS

Describe the last time you were sad:

_____

How did you experience sadness in your mind? _____

How did you experience sadness in your body? _____

How did you respond when you were sad?

_____

What did your sadness tell you about your environment or yourself?

_____

What are unhealthy ways you respond to sadness? _____

What are healthy ways you respond to sadness? _____

FEAR

Describe the last time you were afraid:

_____

How did you experience fear in your mind? _____

How did you experience fear in your body? _____

How did you respond when you were afraid?

_____

What did your fear tell you about your environment or yourself?

_____

What are unhealthy ways you respond to fear? _____

What are healthy ways you respond to fear? _____

TRIGGER	LIMITING BELIEF	EMOTION FELT	WHERE IN MY BODY IS IT FELT	MY BEHAVIOR/ RESPONSE	STRESS SKILL I CAN USE	RESOLUTION TO TRIGGER EVENT
EXAMPLES *Did poorly on quiz*	*I am a failure*	*Fear, shame*	*Stomach*	*Shut down, lose motivation to try*	*Deep breathing*	*I created a plan to stay on top of my coursework*

HAPPINESS HABITS

Happiness Habits are healthy, long-term actions that cause your brain to release happiness hormones including endorphins, dopamine, serotonin, and oxytocin. Happiness Habits help you stay in your upstairs brain, where you access the problem-solving skills, collaboration, and passion critical for hope.

Positive Feelings

Positive feelings, the first ingredient of hope, are feelings that are located in your upstairs brain like wonder, joy, and peace that make it easier to overcome obstacles that get in the way of hope. You proactively manage the emotional despair of hopelessness using Stress Skills and use your Happiness Habits to stay in your upstairs brain, where you then energetically move towards your goals in life.

Activating purpose	Exercising / Nutrition	Volunteering
Pursuing passion	Creating / listening to music	Wonder/Awe
Utilizing strengths	Dancing / Singing	Quality sleep
Meditation	Drawing / Painting	Doodling
Smiling	Gratitude	

HAPPINESS HABITS

Directions: Circle your top four favorite happiness habits from the list below. If there are additional happiness habits you use that are not on the list, use the space below the add them.

- Setting SMART goals
- Practicing gratitude
- Practicing kindness
- Thinking about positive things that make us happy
- Exercising
- Starting the day right (even just making the bed)
- Eating healthy foods like fruits and vegetables
- Walking outside
- Focusing on faith
- Playing an instrument
- Singing

- Experiencing wonder or awe
- Being creative
- Taking photos
- Drawing or painting
- Dancing
- Doing jumping jacks
- Skipping
- Playing games
- Listening to happy music
- Spending time with friends
- Volunteering
- Any other positive actions that make you happy

My favorite happiness habits:

-
-
-
-
-
-
-
-

HAPPINESS **HABITS**

The Second Key to Shine Hope is activating hope using Happiness Habits.
Happiness Habits are healthy, long-term actions that cause your brain to release endorphins, dopamine, serotonin, and oxytocin. Happiness Habits help you stay in your upstairs brain, where you access the problem-solving skills, collaboration, and passion critical for hope.

Like Stress Skills, different Happiness Habits work for different people. Therefore, it's important that you try numerous Happiness Habits to find the ones that most successfully help you stay in your upstairs brain.

PRACTICING HAPPINESS HABITS

Take time to practice at least one new Happiness Habit each day this week. When life gets busy, it can be tempting to skip your Happiness Habits. However, it is important to practice Happiness Habits every day, especially when you are stressed. Happiness Habits combat the negative impact of stress hormones and help us maintain the hopeful mindset we need to navigate challenging times.

What Happiness Habits did you practice this week?

1. _____

2. _____

3. _____

4. _____

5. _____

6. _____

7. _____

Which Happiness Habits did you enjoy the most? Why?

_____

_____

_____

_____

Think about one of the Happiness Habit you enjoyed the most, and answer the following questions:

How did your body feel before practicing your Happiness Habit?

_____

_____

How did your body feel during your Happiness Habit?

_____

_____

How did your body feel after practicing your Happiness Habit?

_____

_____

How did the Happiness Habit impact your beliefs? Thoughts?

_____

_____

Was there a day that you didn't feel like you had time for a Happiness Habit? How did it feel to make time for it anyways?

_____

_____

_____

_____

HAPPINESS HABITS: GRATITUDE

This exercise is an excerpt from Dr. Dan Tomasulo's book, "Learned Hopefulness." Take five minutes to write down everything that happened yesterday. Pay attention to what happened, how it made you feel, and how you responded. Focus on your thoughts and feelings during your reflection.

Gratitude is one of the Happiness Habits that can help us stay in our upstairs brain. Take the next five minutes to once again write down everything that happened yesterday, but now, frame it through the lens of gratitude. What were you grateful for? When things didn't go as you wanted or you were triggered, what could you find to still be grateful for?

INSPIRED ACTIONS

Inspired Actions, the second ingredient of hope, are the deliberate steps you take toward your goals in life. Inspired Actions help you to move away from the motivational helplessness, the second ingredient of hopelessness, and toward what you are hopeful for in life.

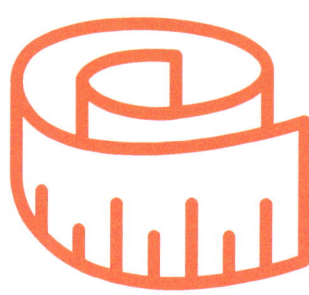

Types of Goals:

WOOP	SMART
Achievement	Stretch
Intrinsic	Micro-Goals

Pathways, Agency, and Regoaling

Obstacles are inevitable, and sometimes you can't reach the goal as you intended. It is important to embrace obstacles to goals, learn to pivot or reevaluate, be flexible and adaptable, and never be afraid to ask for help.

If a goal seems too big, use the stepping process or create micro-goals to chunk it down into smaller goals. Think of one thing you can do in the next 20 minutes. And know when you need to re-goal.

S.M.A.R.T. Goals

 **S**PECIFIC

Be specific about your goal. Think about these questions when creating your goal: What needs to be accomplished? Who is responsible for it? What steps will you take to achieve it?

 **M**EASURABLE

Can you measure your progress? If this goal will take a long time to achieve, set shorter term goals to reach along the way.

 **A**CHIEVABLE

Are you inspired and motivated to reach your goal? Do you have the tools or skills you need? If not, do you know how you can get them?

 **R**ELEVANT

Does your goal go along with what you are trying to achieve in the future? Is it important to you? Is it something you care about?

 **T**IME-BOUND

Is your timing realistic? Can you achieve your goal in the time period set? Think about what you may want to achieve at the halfway point.

INSPIRED **ACTIONS**

The Third Key to Shine Hope is taking Inspired Actions using a variety of goal-setting techniques. Inspired actions, the second ingredient of hope, are the actions that we take as we move from hopelessness towards what we want in life. Inspired Actions help you to move away from the motivational helplessness, the second ingredient of hopelessness, and toward what you are hopeful for in life.

GOAL SETTING WITH HOPE

Goal setting is an important part of the Hope Matrix. Even if we don't reach our goals, the simple act of setting the goal and working towards it can help us maintain a Hopeful Mindset. Therefore, don't let yourself lose hope if you have to change or update your goals.

Hope is a vision for the future, fueled by positive feelings and inspired actions. Therefore, if you want to set goals with hope, it's important to set **achievement goals,** not avoidance goals. Achievement goals are created based on what we want to obtain, while avoidance goals are created based on things we don't want to happen. For example, if you are focused on fitness, set goals like "I will finish the marathon," rather than "I won't quit halfway through the marathon."

It is also important to set **intrinsic goals**, rather than extrinsic goals. Extrinsic goals pertain to external achievements, such as wealth, power, or fame, and are associated with anxiety, depression, and lower happiness. Intrinsic goals, on the other hand, are goals that pertain to your passions and core values, and are always focused on one of three things: meaningful relationships, personal growth, or community contributions. Intrinsic goals are positively associated with well-being, happiness, and high psychological health.

For example, if you are setting a goal for exercise, an intrinsic goal would be "I will exercise to feel healthier" rather than "I will exercise to impress others."

You can begin to brainstorm goals using the **WOOP Framework**. The WOOP Framework includes four steps: **W**(wish), **O**(outcome), **O**(obstacle), and **P**(plan):

W**ISH:** Think about what you want in life. Pick a wish that is challenging but that you can still fulfill.

O**UTCOME:** What would be the best possible outcome if your wish came true? How would fulfilling your wish make you feel?

O**BSTACLE:** What is within you or in your environment that keeps you from fulfilling your wish?

P**LAN:** Identify one action you can take or thought you can think to overcome your obstacle. Then, make an if-then plan: IF (I encounter this obstacle) THEN (I will use this solution).

When setting goals, you want to ensure that you are setting **SMART Goals**: Goals that are Specific, Measurable, Attainable, Relevant, and Time-bound. Refer to the SMART Goals poster for more information.

You should always have at least a few **stretch goals** for yourself. Stretch goals are long-term goals that you set to reach your purpose; they should stretch and challenge you, and inspire you to keep moving forward.

For each stretch goal, consider creating some **micro-goals.** Micro-goals are the small, achievable goals that help you move toward your stretch goals. They are the steps in the stepping process that help you continue looking towards the future. And remember- even your micro-goals should be achievement and intrinsic goals, not avoidance and extrinsic goals.

SETTING SMART GOALS USING WOOP

Pick one area of your life (job, health, relationships, etc.).
Brainstorm a goal using WOOP:

WISH _____

OUTCOME _____

OBSTACLE _____

PLAN _____

Based on your WOOP brainstorm, write down a stretch goal on the next page. Check all of the boxes that apply to your goal, then explain how your goal meets each of the criteria. If it doesn't meet one of the criteria, revise your goal and try again.

GOAL:

_____

_____

_____

_____

IS IT: HOW?

   SPECIFIC _____

   MEASURABLE _____

   ACHIEVABLE _____

   RELEVANT _____

   TIME-BOUND _____

Is your goal an achievement goal?   YES   NO

Is your goal an intrinsic goal?   YES   NO

Now, use the stepping method to come up with five microgoals that will help you reach your goal

1 _____

2 _____

3 _____

4 _____

5 _____

What is a stretch goal you would like to work toward?

_____

_____

_____

_____

REFLECTION

How can your strengths help you pick and set goals?

_____

_____

What strengths can you rely on to overcome obstacles?

_____

_____

What other areas of your life might you want to set goals for?

_____

_____

What are some goals you could set?

_____

_____

GOAL SETTING

Use this worksheet regularly in your goal setting process. Feel free to copy and complete for multiple goals, including family, relationships, health, and community. And remember to set some stretch goals, which takes you beyond the SMART process.

MY SMART GOAL: ( )

IS IT:

SPECIFIC

MEASURABLE

ACHIEVABLE

RELEVANT

TIME-BOUND

NO, IT'S A
STRETCH GOAL! :)

Is your goal an achievement goal?

YES   NO

Is your goal an intrinsic goal?

YES   NO

What are the feelings associated with achieving this goal?

_____

_____

_____

_____

What positive affirmation am I willing to say daily to achieve this goal?

_____

_____

_____

_____

Why do you want to achieve this goal?

_____

_____

_____

_____

To support this goal, I commit to regular practice of:

Three Stress Skills	Three Happiness Habits	Eliminating These Challenges
_____	_____	_____
_____	_____	_____
_____	_____	_____

What are six steps or microgoals that will help me reach my SMART goal?

1 _____   4 _____

2 _____   5 _____

3 _____   6 _____

Name 3 obstacles towards my smart goals:

Name multiple ways to overcome each obstacle:

1 _____   _____

2 _____   _____

3 _____   _____

_____

Name one person I can check in regularly on this goal:

Contact this person now and make a regular appointment to check in:

_____   DONE!

What step can I take in the next five minutes to get closer to my goal.

_____

_____

NOURISHING NETWORKS

Your Nourishing Networks, also known as your Hope Networks, are the people in your life that provide you with support, help you stay on track, encourage you to succeed, and who you do the same for in return. You are up to 95% more likely to achieve a goal if you write it down, and check in with someone regularly. So Nourishing Networks are critical support systems for moving you towards what you hope for in life.

Your Hope Networks should include:

People who know and understand you.

People who value your strengths.

People who activate the SHINE framework.

People whom you trust and can confide in.

People who are available to support you.

People you are willing to do the above for as well.

Enhancing Your Hope Networks

Enhance your Hope Networks using the 5:1 rule, vulnerability, praise, recognition, kindness, gratitude, empathy, compassion, collaboration, and strong communication, and be sure to have different networks for different areas of life.

Don't forget to include doctors, therapists, and/or other medical professionals in your Hope Networks.

NOURISHING **NETWORKS**

The Fourth Key to Shine Hope is creating and cultivating strong Nourishing Networks. Your Nourishing Networks, also known as your Hope Networks, are the people in your life that provide you with support, help you stay on track, encourage you to succeed, and who you do the same for in return.

You are up to 95% more likely to achieve a goal if you write it down, and check in with someone regularly. So Nourishing Networks are critical support systems for moving you towards what you want in life.

Begin to brainstorm the people who belong in your Hope Networks and where they fit:

Friends and Family I count on:

_____

_____

People I turn to for Stress Skills:

_____

_____

People I practice Happiness Habits with:

_____

_____

Things I can connect to: *ex. Spiritual Advisor, Peer Support, Colleagues, Pets, Nature*

_____

_____

Medical experts I can turn to when I need help:

_____

_____

Community resources I can utilize:

_____

_____

Where can I go in times of crisis?
ex. If you can't list anyone, you can check out our list of resources for how to get connected.
Scan QR Code on Page 44.

_____

_____

STRENGTHENING YOUR HOPE NETWORK

Now that you've identified some of the people in your Hope Networks, how can you strengthen those relationships? You can enhance your Hope Networks using the 5:1 rule, vulnerability, praise, recognition, kindness, gratitude, empathy, compassion, collaboration, and strong communication.

The 5:1 rule states that for every one negative or constructive criticism you say to someone, you should say five positive things. Pick one person from your Hope Networks and write down five things you love about them. Once you've written down all five, call or text the person you chose and tell them all five things.

1 _____
2 _____
3 _____
4 _____
5 _____

Who is one person I can go to in a time of need?

⌜_____⌝

Remember, the size of your Hope Network doesn't matter, the quality of your connections matters. **The best way to receive support is to give support.**

ELIMINATING CHALLENGES

Challenges to Hope are negative habits of thought that quickly take you to hopelessness, that emotional despair and sense of helplessness. The thought patterns are often unconscious habits, so becoming aware of these patterns is critical. Once we know what they are and recognize them, it is important to counteract them so that we don't let them keep us from all we hope for in life.

Eliminating Challenges

Most of the Challenges to Hope take constant, repetitive actions to change and overcome. Thanks to the science of neuroplasticity, we know it is possible with practice and dedication. The key is to learn to identify what specific challenges happen most frequently and then proactively find ways to manage those challenges.

Limiting beliefs	Focusing on Uncontrollables	Mind Wandering
Automatic Negative Thoughts (ANTs)	Attaching to outcomes	Implicity Bias
All-or-nothing thinking	Internalizing failure	Negative Framing
Negative bias	Toxic Consumption	Perfectionism
Rumination & Worry	Nocebo Effect	Taking things personally

ELIMINATING **CHALLENGES**

The Fifth Key to Shine Hope is Eliminating the Challenges. Challenges to Hope are negative habits of thought that quickly take you to hopelessness, that emotional despair and sense of helplessness. The thought patterns are often unconscious habits we don't realize we're doing, so becoming aware of these patterns is critical. Once we know what they are and recognize them, it is important to counteract them so that we don't let them keep us from all we hope for in life.

CHALLENGE #1: LIMITING BELIEFS Limiting beliefs are negative thoughts or opinions that we tell ourselves are true that keep us in a negative mindset. They are at the core of our anxieties, fears, and insecurities. In order to truly create, maintain, and grow hope, we must first identify the limiting beliefs we have around hope and find ways to overcome them.

CHALLENGE #2: AUTOMATIC NEGATIVE THOUGHTS (ANTs) Automatic negative thoughts (ANTs) are repetitive negative thoughts that we form instantaneously in response to external stimuli. They're often hurtful or irrational, and can send us into a spiral of hopelessness if not managed.

CHALLENGE #3: ALL-OR-NOTHING THINKING All-or-nothing thinking is a negative thought pattern in which we only think in extremes. Rather than seeing all of the solutions to a problem, all-or-nothing thinking forces us to only see either complete success or complete failure.

CHALLENGE #4: NEGATIVE BIAS Negativity bias refers to the psychological phenomenon that causes negative events to have a greater impact on our brains than positive ones. We tend to fixate on a criticism rather than a compliment, pay more attention to bad news than good news, and notice negative events happening near us instead of positive ones. Negativity bias forces us into our downstairs brain, and can have lasting impacts on our relationships, behavior, and hope.

CHALLENGE #5: RUMINATION Rumination refers to when we repeatedly go over a thought or a problem from the past in our heads, without end. Rumination is associated with numerous negative mental states, including depression, anxiety, post-traumatic stress disorder, and hopelessness.

CHALLENGE #6: WORRY Worry is when we feel anxious or afraid about real or imagined future scenarios. Where rumination focuses on the past, worry focuses on the future. Worry forces us to fixate on and respond to future danger that we think we may encounter.

CHALLENGE #7: FOCUSING ON UNCONTROLLABLES Focusing on Uncontrollables is when you focus on things that are outside of your influence of power. This can lead to rumination and worry, which in turn can cause stress, anxiety, and depression. It is important to proactively manage what you can control and learn to release the rest.

CHALLENGE #8: ATTACHING TO OUTCOMES Attaching to outcomes is when we set goals, and are then unable or willing to be satisfied unless we reach that specific goal. While goal setting is important, it is also important to have a sense of active surrender and know that sometimes there is a better path. Being too attached to specific goal attainment leads to hopelessness when we don't reach that goal.

CHALLENGE #9: INTERNALIZING FAILURE There is actually a biological link between failure and your physical and mental health. When we achieve our goals, our brains release testosterone and dopamine, and we experience positive feelings. Science has found that, with time and repetition, these chemicals can alter the chemistry of our brains in positive ways.

The opposite is also true. If we fail early while others succeed, we are more likely to make future mistakes if, instead of learning from the failure, we let it affect our feeling state and future confidence.

To overcome this biological response and hopelessness cycle, the key is to learn how to not internalize failure. See, failure is an indication that one of the steps in your process failed, not that **you** failed. And once you learn to deconstruct the process, you can end failure.

ELIMINATING CHALLENGES PRACTICE: FOCUSING ON THE CONTROLLABLES

In the sunflower below, write down the things you can control. In the areas around the sunflower, write down the things you cannot control. It's important to focus on things inside the sunflower and find ways to release the stress and worry associated with the things outside of the sunflower.

THINGS THAT I CAN CONTROL

THINGS THAT I CANNOT CONTROL

MEASURING YOUR HOPE

Now that you have reached the end of the course, take a moment to retake the Snyder Hope Scale to find your new Hope Score.

Use the link provided to take the Snyder Hope Scale Assessment:

www.theshinehopecompany.com/measure-your-hope

My initial Snyder Hope Scale Score: _____ /64

My Current Snyder Hope Scale Score: _____ /64

Did your score increase or decrease?

_____

_____

What positively or negatively impacted your score?

_____

_____

Remember, your hope score will rise and fall as you go throughout your life. The score is simply a way for you to check in with yourself and keep yourself centered and focused on your hope journey.

☀ MY HOPE HERO

HOW HOPEFUL ARE YOU?

Did you measure your hope? The lower your score, the more you want to practice these skills! Remember, hope is a muscle we need to build it (add it).

Check out here to get your hope score.

To write your hope hero journey, spend 20% of your time writing about their challenge, and 80% of the time sharing strategies for how they overcame it so others can learn from it. Here's how:

 1. Write your hope hero's name in the yellow line next to the box (feel free to use a nickname or anything else).

2. Put your favorite photo of them on the yellow box, or an image of something that represents your hope hero.

3. Write an introduction explaining the challenge they faced. Explain the two ingredients of hopelessness: despair (feelings) and helplessness (inability to act) they experienced.

4. Share sadness, anger, fear, or other feelings, and choose 3 **Stress Skills** they used to navigate them (from the Shine infographic, or choose your own!).

5. Share 3 **Happiness Habits** they used to get back to upstairs brain.

6. Talk about 3 **Inspired Actions** they took, or share how your hope hero chunked down goals, the types of goals they've set, or if they had to regoal.

7. Share who was in their **Nourishing Network**, and how it helped them navigate the challenge.

8. Pick 3 challenges from the '**Eliminating Challenges**' on the infographic, and share how your hope hero eliminated them.

9. Write the conclusion. What do you want the world to know? What do you wish someone had told you? What is the moral of the story?

If you're inspired, share this hope hero story so we can help activate these skills globally!

#Hope #ShineHope #MyHopeHero

> We all experience moments of hopelessness (emotional despair and motivational helplessness). The key is to use the Shine Hope skills to navigate your way from despair to positive feelings, and helplessness to inspired actions. Use the Shine Hope framework to build your muscle.

THE HOPE MATRIX

 **Kathryn Goetzke**

When Kathryn was 18 years old, a freshman at the University of Iowa, her dad died by suicide. It really changed her life. When she was in her early 20's, she then tried to take her own life, yet didn't tell another soul for 10 years. She knows a lot about hopelessness.

 To work on her recovery, she used a lot of Stress Skills. She talks about crying, going to therapy, learning to meditate, deep breathing, and listening to music. She traveled a lot, and took up hiking and exercise. She also took up boxing and spent a lot of time in nature.

 Kathryn was diligent about her Happiness Habits. She listened to her favorite band the Killers, went to concerts, focused on her nutrition and sleep, and started exercising. She pursued her passions, started a nonprofit iFred, and did a lot of volunteer work. She got serious about her purpose.

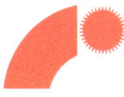 Kathryn also took a lot of Inspired Actions towards her goals. She chunked them down, got a degree and then an MBA. She couldn't talk to her dad anymore, so she found business mentors. Her brothers were always there to support her, and her mom was a source of strength and inspiration.

 Kathryn spent a lot of time with her Nourishing Networks. She spent time with people that were kind, compassionate, fun, and helped her heal. She had a therapist and got close to God. She had animals and spent a lot of time with wild horses in Nevada.

 She worked to Eliminate Challenges like her rumination and worry. She learned about sensory engagement, and even started a company to teach others. She worked to forgive herself and others. She focused on what she could control, which was her present and future, and did her best to let go of the rest. She put all her failures into teaching others.

Her use of the Shine Hope framework led her on a much healthier path. She has been sober almost 20 years, and had her nonprofit that same amount of time. She is a representative at the United Nations for the World Federation for Mental Health, and has shared her story around the world at places like the World Bank, Harvard, the United Nations, and more. She has created programming to teach hope to kids, published papers, and is now doing workplace programming, has a college, course, and is activating cities. She is on a mission to ensure all know how to hope, one person at a time. She is an inspiration, and someone that truly lives by example practicing all she teaches.

#Hope #ShineHope #MyHopeHero

MY HOPE HERO

46

MY SHINE HOPE STORY™

HOW HOPEFUL ARE YOU?
Did you measure your hope? The lower your score, the more you want to practice these skills! Remember, hope is a muscle we need to build it (add it).

 **Check out here to get your hope score.**

To write your own shine hope story, spend 20% of your time writing about your challenge, and 80% of the time sharing strategies for how you overcame it so others can learn from you. Here's how:

1. Write your name in the yellow line next to the box (feel free to use a nickname or anything else).

2. Put your favorite photo on the yellow box, or an image of something that represents you.

3. Write an introduction to your story explaining the challenge you faced. Explain the two ingredients of hopelessness: despair (feelings) and helplessness (inability to act) you experienced.

 4. Share sadness, anger, fear, or other feelings, and choose **3 Stress Skills** you used to naviate them (from the Shine infographic, or choose your own!).

 5. Share **3 Happiness Habits** you used to get back to your upstairs brain.

 6. Talk about **3 Inspired Actions** you took, or share how you chunked down goals, the types of goals you set, or if you had to regoal.

 7. Share who was in your **Nourishing Network**, and how they helped you navigate the challenge.

 8. Pick 3 challenges from the **'Eliminating Challenges'** on the infographic, and share how you eliminated them.

9. Write your conclusion. What do you want the world to know? What do you wish someone had told you? What is the moral of the story?

If you're inspired, share your story so we can help activate these skills globally.

#Hope #ShineHope #MyShineHopeStory

We all experience moments of hopelessness (emotional despair and motivational helplessness). The key is to use the Shine Hope skills to navigate your way from despair to positive feelings, and helplessness to inspired actions. Use the Shine Hope framework to build your muscle.

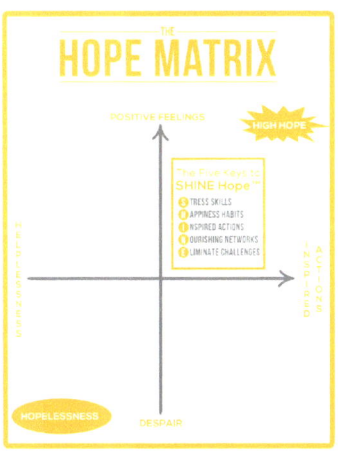

 ## Kathryn Goetzke

When I was 18 years old, a freshman at the University of Iowa, I called home and heard an unfamiliar, deep voice on the other line. It wasn't anyone I recognized, and he asked for my mom. My mom got on the phone to tell me my dad had taken his life. In that instance, my whole world crumbled. I felt a sadness so deep I thought I would never survive, and a helplessness so profound as I could not bring him back.

As hard as it was, I had to move forward. I started using Stress Skills to manage my pain. I cried when I was sad, started boxing to manage my anger, and learned how to start belly breathing to manage my fear. I listened to a lot of calming music when things got hard, and I started hiking all over the world. I also learned how to use sensory engagement to bring myself to the present moment.

Happiness Habits were critical. Sleep became an important part of my routine, and I started eating healthier foods. I cut alcohol out of my life. I replaced smoking with running, and made comedy clubs and laughter a part of my life. I listened to music, turned my sensory engagement passion into a purpose and started a company, and made volunteering a regular part of my life. I used dancing and live concerts (like my fave The Killers) as a form of release.

I also was very intentional about Inspired Actions. I had to chunk down my goals, leaving school and taking only one year at a time until I graduated. I had to regoal from having experiences with my dad to finding father-like figures to be in my life. I got closer to my brothers, their kids, and found mentors like Paul Carter and Dr. Belfer to guide me on my journey. My mom is my rock, my greatest source of strength and inspiration, keeping me moving forward towards my dreams.

Nourishing Networks were a constant. I stayed close to my friends and family, traveling, dancing, studying, and laughing. They were so compassionate, kind, generous, fun, and helped me heal. I forgave my dad for leaving, and forgave myself for not being there for him when he needed me. I got very close to God, understanding that I couldn't save my dad, and that in time this lesson would teach me how to help others.

It wasn't easy to Eliminate Challenges like rumination, internalizing failure, or worry. Yet I studied sensory engagement to be present when my mind started running. I deconstructed what led to my dad taking his life in a way that made it clear how to save myself and others. I knew that I couldn't control my dad, just like I can't control others. So I have focused on creating programming yet not being attached to if people want to learn it.

It's not been the easiest journey, and takes work. Yet by using the Shine Hope framework I have created a new life that is full of wonder, awe, happiness, adventure, and meaning. A different one than I expected, yet a beautiful one because I was able to dive in my pain, and learn the lessons necessary to teach others. And I use all my dad taught me in business to create a Shine Hope model for the world that ensures all know the what, why, and how of hope. And for that I know he is so very proud.

No matter what life brings, Keep Shining.

#Hope #ShineHope #MyHopeStory

the shine hope company

MY SHINE HOPE STORY™

PLANT SUNFLOWER GARDENS TO SHINE HOPE

Gardening is a great time to practice the Shine Hope Framework, as we have a lot of challenges while planting a garden and we can go from hope to hopelessness pretty quickly. Yet that is a normal part of life, so gardening is an easy place to start practicing these skills.

Say you find some tough ground you need to dig into to plant, you may get frustrated and give up. It is a good time to practice a **Stress Skill** like a 90-second pause or deep breathing, to calm down your stress response. Then try again! You may also notice when others get frustrated and teach them how to use this skill to navigate from their downstairs brain back upstairs.

Eating the sunflower seeds (if ok with your doctor) might be a good way for you to practice your **Happiness Habits.** Sunflower seeds are nutritious, high in choline and selenium, great for brain function and memory. You might also get some exercise planting gardens, and spend time in nature, two other Happiness Habits and great ways to release endorphins.

Planting gardens remind us to take **Inspired Actions** by setting specific goals for the garden. If we want a garden, we need to set a SMART goal about how many flowers, when and where we want the garden, and how we are going to grow the flowers. It is best if we write down the plan, chunk it down into actionable steps, think about obstacles and multiple ways we might overcome them, and check in with someone regularly to ensure progress.

We can cultivate our **Nourishing Networks** by planting gardens with others. That way, if we have challenges while planting, we can face them together and be more creative about overcoming them. And if we don't live by the person we want to plant with, we can both decide to plant and check in regularly on the garden. It is also super fun to plan community gardens, or even fields of sunflowers, and all join together in learning and practicing skills to Shine Hope.

And finally, time to get serious about **Eliminating Challenges**. For example, if our sunflowers die and we fail for a season of planting, it is easy for us to think of ourselves as failures. Yet we aren't failures, our process failed. So deconstruct the process. Did we under or over water? Did we plant at the wrong time of year? Was something wrong with the soil? Did we overwater? It is time to investigate, and instead of ruminating about the sunflowers start figuring out what we can do better to try again next year.

Planting sunflowers is a way to spread the message of hope, as if you put up a Gardens of Hope sign with the website, people can then find the curriculum to learn more about the programs for 'how' to hope. Our program is available around the world, and gardens are a great way to share the message that Hope is Teachable.

HOPE **JOURNAL**

HOPE **JOURNAL**

Hopeful Minds is based on the research that hope is teachable. The aim is to equip all students, teachers, and parents with the tools they need to define, learn, and grow a Hopeful Mind. The Hopeful Minds curriculums and resources are available for download at www.hopefulminds.org/curriculums

The Five-Day Global Hope Challenge is a daily challenge that introduces the Five Keys to Shine Hope that everyone can use to activate hope within their lives and their community. The challenge is ideal for governments, workplaces, schools, and more. Sign-up today at www.hopefulcities.org

Friendship Bench,s mission is to get people out of kufungisisa - depression & anxiety - by creating safe spaces and a sense of belonging in communities to improve mental wellbeing and enhance quality of life. To learn more and request a bench placed in your area, visit www.friendshipbenchzimbabwe.org

Karma Box Project is a community initiative allowing people to give non-perishable food, hygiene products, toiletries, and other useful items to those in need. The boxes are filled up with the goods by anyone in the community and someone in need can take items from the box as needed. To learn more, visit www.karmaboxproject.org

One World Strong Foundation created the ResilienceNet Mobile App, which empowers and provides support to local, regional, and national terrorism prevention practitioners, relevant frontline responders and individual Americans seeking support. To learn more about the One World Strong Foundation and download their app, visit www.oneworldstrong.org/copy-of-how-we-do-it

National Alliance on Mental Illness (NAMI) is America's largest grassroots mental health organization dedicated to building better lives for Americans affected by mental illness. NAMI offers an abundance of resources for those navigating mental illness or for those seeking to learn more. Find more at www.nami.org/home

Choose Love Movement nurtures safer and more loving communities through next generation essential life skills and character development programs for all stages of life. Choose Love is an evidence-based curriculum that will help students feel safer, learn better, and achieve more! Find out more at www.chooselovemovement.org

Hope Means Nevada works to eliminate teen suicide and empower Nevada's youth to live hopeful lives. Find out more at www.hopemeansnevada.org

One Mind catalyzes visionary change through science, business and media to transform the world's mental health. Find out more at www.onemind.org

Charter for Compassion supports the emerging global movement that brings compassion to life. It is a global network connecting people, cities, grassroots organizers and leaders to each other. It provides educational resources, organizing tools, and avenues for communication. Find out more at www.charterforcompassion.org

Hopeful Mindsets®

Hopeful Mindsets® is a framework that uses the Five Keys to Shine Hope to apply to any challenge in life. It is based on the work of leading experts on Hope, Mindset, Mental Health, Stress, Positive Psychology, Business, Communications, and more. Using the Five Keys to Shine Hope as a foundation, Hopeful Mindsets introduces critical hope skills to help anyone move from hopelessness to hope.

The initial program, Hopeful Mindsets on the College Campus, is a 10-module video course from The Shine Hope Company that equips students with crucial hope skills through expert insights and real-life stories. The course features experts from Harvard, Stanford, and Columbia, with insights from recent college graduates that offer real-life practical strategies and stories from their experiences with homelessness, mental health diagnoses, death, violence, and everyday challenges at school.

The Hopeful Mindsets General Overview is a 90-minute video course for anyone that introduces hope and the Five Keys to Shine Hope framework to help you create, maintain, and grow hope in your life. This course is taught by Kathryn Goetzke, based on her knowledge of mental health and hope, and her work to date. It compiles knowledge from leading experts on Hope, Mindset, Mental Health, Stress, Positive Psychology, Business, Communications, and includes video lessons, a full downloadable workbook and exercises to practice skills for hope, and is available individually or to license for organizations.

The Hopeful Mindsets Workplace Overview is a 90-minute video course for the workplace that introduces hope and the Five Keys to Shine Hope™ framework to help you create, maintain, and grow hope in the workplace. We give an overview of the framework, so you can then apply it to your career to activate hope at work. The course is available for individuals or to license to entire companies, to ensure all know the what, why, and how of hope.

You can learn more about the Hopeful Mindsets courses at **www.hopecourses.com.**

☀️Hopeful Cities®

Hopeful Cities® is equipping cities around the world with the tools they need to create, maintain, and grow hope, citywide. Learn how you can activate hope in your community at **www.hopefulcities.org.**

 ## Hopeful Minds

Hopeful Minds® is programming for youth based on research that suggests hope is teachable (a skill). The aim is to equip students, teachers, and parents with the tools they need to define, learn, and grow Hopeful Minds in young kids. Learn more at **www.hopefulminds.org.**

 the
shine hope™
company

The Shine Hope Company™ - Our mission is to improve lives globally by teaching scientifically informed and evidence-based methods to measure and cultivate hope. Learn how to activate hope in your life and community at **www.theshinehopecompany.com.**

If you are in need of support, you can find additional resources by visiting **www.ifred.org/individual-support** or scanning the QR Code.

This workbook was created by The Shine Hope Company. It is intended to accompany the Hopeful Mindsets Overview Course, which can be purchased at www.hopecourses.com. The Hopeful Mindsets Overview Course is not included in the purchase of this workbook.